Pocket guide

Working from Home

LAWPACK

Pocket guide

Working from Home

by Hugh Williams FCA

The author

Hugh Williams is the author of bestselling Lawpack titles on self-employment and tax; while he is a director of Help4Business Ltd., he is also founding partner of HM Williams Chartered Accountants based in Plymouth, a firm that has won several national awards.

Working from Home
by Hugh Williams

© 2005 Lawpack Publishing Limited
Lawpack Publishing Limited
76–89 Alscot Road
London SE1 3AW

www.lawpack.co.uk

ISBN: 1 904053 79 3

The law is stated as at 1 April 2005

Valid in England & Wales and Scotland

Exclusion of Liability and Disclaimer

Parts of this book have been reproduced from *Self-Employment Kit* and *Tax Answers at a Glance* both by Hugh Williams, and from *Running Your Own Business Made Easy* by Roy Hedges, all published by Lawpack.

Contents

Introduction

So, you have decided to work from home. Good for you! While this may or may not be a matter of choice in your case, speaking as someone who worked from home for more than 30 years, I can definitely recommend it, whatever the reasons for it.

There are a few disadvantages, but these are heavily outweighed by the advantages and one of the main thrusts of this Pocket Guide is to encourage you as you develop (what may be) a wholly new mode of working as you get going at home. Yes, I will be looking at the legal aspects to try to help you become aware of how the law will affect your new circumstances, but my aim is not to knock you down with a whole lot of legal 'Thou shalt nots!'. Instead, I will be explaining how to keep them in their proper perspective.

This book is meant to be (what it appears at first glance) a light read which, while telling you of the pitfalls to beware of, encourages you to make the most of all the opportunities that this new development in your life presents.

So, what is it that has brought you to working at home?

There seem to be two types of people who work from home:

1. The self-employed who set up a business (however small) at home.

2. Employees who either ask if they can or are asked if they are prepared to carry out their duties at home.

It seems to me that in the case of employees the rules they need to know are much less numerous, indeed less onerous, than in the case of the self-employed. There are, as you would expect, a number of issues that overlap both types of homeworking, but the main burden, that of being aware of the rules which affect those who work from home, falls more on the self-employed. So, it is with them that I will start and I will deal with employees who work from home later.

Hugh Williams
April 2005

CHAPTER 1

Starting off

Having the right attitude

There are two things to bear in mind when starting a business at home:

1. Are you trying to create a business that, one day, will be valuable and therefore potentially saleable or are you simply wanting to earn a small subsidiary income?

2. Are you aware that running a small business from home is not a game? There will be certain responsibilities you will have to embrace. You must be aware of what they are (my aim is to include them in this book) and you must carry them out.

In other words, this is a serious move. I want you to succeed and, if you are to, you will need to plan, from the outset, to create a business that will achieve your aims and one that will not get you into trouble with the law.

But how can you tell if you have the right attitude? Why not try the following self-assessment test and find out if you are made of the right stuff to run your own business?

Use the questionnaire to discover to what degree you possess these needed traits. Be honest with yourself when answering the questions. Nothing is gained by being untruthful; the only person you hurt is yourself.

Read each question or statement carefully. Reflect on how strongly you either agree or disagree with it. Show how you identify with each remark by scoring from 1 to 10 at the end of each statement. For example, 1 will indicate that you disagree with the question whereas 10 will signify that you strongly agree, i.e. it is intended that your answer will sum up your character precisely with regard to each question.

So, just to double-check with you, in respect of the question 'Do I perform well under pressure?', if you concur that you do perform well when under pressure, enter 10. If you feel your work deteriorates under pressure, enter 1. If you believe working under pressure makes you feel uncomfortable, but your work doesn't suffer, enter 4, etc.

Score each question out of 10:

1. Do I perform well under pressure?

2. Do I stay calm and not get stressed?

3. Do I persevere when influences over which I have no control affect my life?

4. Can I work with, and lead, a team?

5. Am I prepared to make a plan for the future of my business and to revisit it regularly to see how things are turning out against this plan?

6. Does making decisions come easily?

7. Are the decisions I make usually the right ones?

8. Am I positive, and do I enjoy taking risks?

9. Am I prepared to delegate the work my business does to employees, so that I can concentrate on managing the business?

10. Do I work well using my own initiative?

11. Do I bounce back from setbacks and work at a problem until it is solved?

12. Does the thought of learning new skills and the responsibility of being my own boss excite me?

13. Do I have the ability to change my mind when it is obvious an earlier decision was wrong?

14. Does explaining things to others come easily, and am I patient if I am misunderstood?

15. How much may my spouse/partner object to my business interfering with our private lives? (no objection = 10)

16. Am I a good listener, and can I take advice from others?

17. Do I prefer to stand alone, than to be one of a crowd?

18. Do I enjoy meeting and dealing with different people?

19. Is having my success recognised by others important to me? (not important = 10)

20. Am I at present in good health, and rarely get sick?

When you have answered all of the questions and statements, total your score. Look below to see how you shape up to becoming an entrepreneur. If you are in doubt, give your completed assessment questionnaire to a friend or relation you trust. Ask him for a fair appraisal of your abilities. Don't be afraid of criticism. Learning to accept your faults is another trait you'll need in your armoury. Learning to conquer your failings is the bedrock of successful businesses.

Assessment results

Look for the group into which your score falls. In addition, also reconsider any scores which were either extremely high or low; assess how accurate you have been.

180 to 200 If your score lies in this band, stress and pressure spur you on. You are dedicated and prepared to work hard to achieve your goals. The risk and insecurity of running your own business will motivate rather than worry you. You have every chance of success with the right business idea and sound planning.

140 to 179 Certain aspects of running your own business may give you problems. The severity of these will depend on your determination to overcome adversity. Concentrate on improving those areas where you did not have a high score. However, you seem to have the right frame of mind to deal with the day-to-day pressures of running a business. Your business should flourish and you'll probably enjoy the rewards more than those with a higher score.

100 to 139 If your scores varied wildly, such as a lot of 1, 2, 8 and 9s, you must try to improve the lower scores. Otherwise, those regions could be the source of severe problems if you are unable to change them. If this score was reached with reasonably consistent scoring, you should have no cause for concern, but you must ensure that you have a good business plan and are prepared to make use of the various training schemes.

60 to 99 If your responses were born out of uncertainty, contact your local enterprise agency for details of training courses. While you may have the ability to run your own business, there are strong indications that you will not enjoy it. Not enjoying your business could cause you to give up under the slightest pressure. Think long and hard about whether you really want to run a business. If you still think going into business is for you, make use of the help and training that are readily available.

Under 60 Running your own business will be a strain – one you may not wish to endure for long. Running a business requires confidence, self-reliance and the competence to handle stress and pressure. Without these traits it would be unwise to set up your own business. You should find out about training courses in your local area to develop the skills you lack.

The above assessment is not an appraisal of your technical and commercial proficiency, but of your personal attributes, which could affect your business. It's basic and is only intended to give a broad idea of your aptitude. Contact your local Business Link for details of courses in your area, since even with the right personality and attitude, some skills instruction may be beneficial.

Making a business plan

I want to put your mind at rest over the need to have a business plan at the outset. I don't think you need go to the extent and expense of preparing a long and detailed business plan – unless your bank asks you to do so. If you want to, by all means do, and I include a sample business plan in Appendix 4.

No, what I think you should do is, using no more than one side of a sheet of A4 paper, write out what you are planning to do and what you hope to achieve.

It could be a single sentence that reads 'In five years' time I would like to have created a business that brings me in a net profit of £30,000 per year, preferably one in which I don't need to do all the work and that I might be able to sell.'.

Obviously it's a good idea to say where this income is going to come from (e.g. selling your services as a consultant, making wedding dresses, writing books, etc.) and it is very important (as well as giving you reassurance that it may happen) to prepare a little table that looks something like this:

	No. of Customers	Average Value of Each Sale	Average No. of Times They Buy	Sales Income £	Materials Bought £	Over-heads £	Profit £
	A	B	C	(=AxBxC) D	E	F	Profit = D–E–F
Year 1	10	250	1	2,500	500	1,000	1,000
Year 2	20	275	1.5	8,250	1,650	2,000	4,600
Year 3	30	303	2	18,180	3,630	4,000	10,550
Year 4	40	333	2.5	33,300	6,655	8,000	18,645
Year 5	50	366	3	54,900	10,981	16,000	27,919

Working from Home

Having done this, you should show it to someone you trust and whose views you respect so he can let you know what he thinks.

From experience, I can assure you that it is very important to prepare a plan (as the example above) as it can show very readily whether you are likely to succeed.

Businesses are most likely to fail during the early years of trading, with 20 per cent of new business shutting down in the first year. As a result, you may also want to consider the other following factors, if they are appropriate to your situation, which may help suggest whether your business is viable:

- Have I done in-depth market research? Find out as much as possible about your potential and existing customers.

- Do I have a plan on how to attract the customers I am expecting?

- Do I have a financial contingency plan for times of need (e.g. interest rates may rise and this may affect your cashflow)? Build up your cash reserves.

- Have I made a realistic forecast? There is no point in being too optimistic. Focus on growing the size of sales rather than on profit, and don't diversify into unknown areas too soon.

- Have I prepared a budget to plan how to spend and save my money? Do include a personal budget setting limits on the amounts you need for domestic expenditure.

- Am I monitoring the competition enough? Do make sure that you notice any possible threats to your business.

- Are my products competitively priced and reliable, and are my credit arrangements adequate? Do carry out credit checks on potential and existing customers.

Indeed, should, for whatever reason, your business fail, if you can show those involved in helping you sort things out that you were methodical and realistic and had a viable plan at the outset, they will be far more sympathetic to your cause than if you appear to have done no planning.

Raising finance

If you don't have enough money to kick-start your business, you may need to raise some. Here are some ideas for sources you could approach:

- Your family.

- Your bank.

- Small Firms Loan Guarantee – via your bank (see page 9).

- Leasing and hire purchase. However, beware of the pitfalls; for example, under a lease or HP agreement, you are committed to a certain minimum period of monthly payments and if you want to end the contract early, there will almost certainly be a penalty to pay.

- Venture capital – again there are pitfalls, such as those who provide the money will want to keep a close tab on how their investment is performing and you may not like them interfering too much.

- Grants – Business Link (see page 17).

- Pension funds and insurance companies.

- Others – the list of individual organisations is very long.

When seeking funding, try to focus on how the loan will be repaid and the expected return your investors will receive. Emphasise your commitment to the business by investing your own money in it. If you have a poor credit rating, come clean, explaining why this arose and what you are doing to try to repair it.

> **? I don't need to raise finance; should I prepare a financial statement?**
>
> *No, but you should have a plan. Why not write it out as I suggest on page 5.*

Seeking Government support

Borrowing money from a bank to start your business will be expensive and there are lots of tales of banks being only 'fair-weather' friends, so another possible source of finance could be a grant from the Government to help with start-up costs.

Now, the Government is not in the business of giving grants to every small business that comes cap-in-hand. There are lots of factors (even limitations) that need to be adhered to.

Most grants are limited to the size of the business (in terms of employees). Location is also an important consideration and being eligible for a grant may mean locating to another part of the country where special financial assistance is targeted.

There is one point about grants which is seldom mentioned, but which is advisable to consider before applying for one. It is that while grants are certainly attractive, they do sometimes bring with them irritating and long-lasting problems. For example, if you are given a grant to build a workshop, it is quite likely that the necessary paper and general bureaucratic work will result in the building taking longer to put up than it would otherwise. You may also have to conform to certain state regulations which you may feel are unnecessary and on top of this many grants are not grants but loans and they have to be repaid if you sell or lease your business.

Generally, though, grants can be valuable, so it's worth checking them out through your nearest Business Link office; ask for its factsheet called *A Guide to Government Grants*.

Using a loan guarantee scheme

Often a business person looking to go self-employed who goes to his bank for a loan is turned down. Not because the bank is unimpressed with the business plan, or unconvinced that the person has the necessary skills; primarily, it will be from insufficient financial security. Banks like to keep their exposure to risk as low as they can and if you don't have the collateral to guarantee the loan, there could be a problem.

However, if you don't have a viable business proposal, there are circumstances where the Government will act as a guarantor. It is called the 'Small Firms Loan Guarantee' and it allows the applicant to get a loan from a normal high-street bank

> **? What is the Small Firms Loan Guarantee?**
>
> *A joint venture between the Department of Trade and Industry, banks and other lenders.*

without giving personal guarantees; the Government acts as the guarantor.

Loans are available from £5,000 to £100,000 (repayable between two and ten years). After two years' trading the loan guarantee can be extended to £250,000.

The business person only needs to finance security to cover 25 per cent of the loan – the Government guarantees the remaining 75 per cent. In return for the guarantee, the Government charges the borrower a premium of two per cent a year on the outstanding amount of the loan.

How to approach a possible lender

The following steps are recommended if finance is being sought from a third party for any new project or business expansion:

1. Assemble up-to-date financial information, including where appropriate:

   - Accounts for the most recent year
   - Management accounts for the current period comparing actual results with budget
   - Profit forecasts for future years
   - Cashflow forecasts
   - Projected balance sheets

   If the latest accounts are out of date, the potential lender is not going to be impressed. See pages 38–43 for guidance on how to understand and manage them correctly.

2. Consult a market research professional for his views on any new product you are considering. These experts see so many products fail and their experience in this field will either confirm or contradict your views and perhaps save you a lot of time and money. The potential lender will be very interested in the result of this research.

3. Arrange an informal meeting with the potential lender at an early stage. Sound him out and, if he shows interest, tell him that a detailed report will be prepared.

4. Consider alternative sources of finance, such as:

   - The sale of unwanted assets

   - Existing cash balances (business or private)

   - Leasing, hire purchase, renting, etc.

5. Prepare a business plan for a potential lender. All reports will differ in content, but the basic format should be one that the lender or an investor finds easy to grasp and you should follow the layout in Appendix 4. Before presenting it, do back up any assumptions you have made in the plan by doing thorough research, as well as find out your own credit rating – you can do this by contacting Experian (www.experian.co.uk) or Equifax (www.equifax.co.uk) and asking for your credit file.

What business structure should I use?

Starting to go self-employed is a major decision in life, and before you jump from whatever you are doing presently into self-employment, it is important to choose the right sort of surface to land on.

Sole proprietor/sole trader

The commonest sort of business is a sole proprietor. Its chief features are as follows:

1. The business person trades under his own name, or under a trading name.

2. The trader keeps his own accounts or employs an accountant and submits financial accounts to the Inland Revenue.

3. It is essentially a very simple structure to operate.

> **❓ As a sole trader, what am I personally liable for in respect of the business?**
>
> *Any debts or losses incurred by the business.*

Partnership

A variation of the sole proprietorship is the partnership. If you have a spouse or friend with whom you wish to enter a business association, then a partnership is the commonest sort of business structure for making this arrangement. In this instance, you should arrange for a solicitor to draw up a partnership deed or you may decide to prepare your own using Lawpack's *Business Partnership Agreement*. Not only does this legal document give a proper foundation to this business relationship, but the deed also forms part of the evidence that the Inland Revenue requires in order to satisfy itself that a partnership is in existence. However, beware of the pitfalls of a partnership – you may be held liable for your partner's debts. Partnerships, like marriage, are not to be entered into lightly.

The golden rules seem to be:

1. While the presence of other people can be a great, if not vital, boon to a business, it is important for there to be one boss and so sharing business responsibilities equally (50:50) is not always the most advisable split to aim for.

2. If someone looks like he would be an ideal business partner, he should be introduced to the partner level slowly, probably by becoming an employee first.

3. Husband and wife partnerships are not usually sensible business arrangements for a variety of reasons, but the most important one being the legal concept of joint and several liability. What this means is that, if a partnership collapses in liquidation, and if one partner cannot pay his

or her share of the debts, the other partner(s) is (are) legally liable for all these debts. So if, for example, a man, who is a partner, loses his all, he will have to pay his share, but his wife's possessions

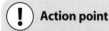

Action point

If you are going into partnership with someone else, have you had a proper legal partnership agreement prepared?

cannot be touched. However, if they are both in partnership, everything they both own will be at risk of being in settlement of the partnership debts.

4. When a partnership is created, be sure to get a proper legal agreement prepared so that, if things go wrong, it has been decided at the outset by both parties in their partnership agreement how the problems are to be resolved. Before going to see a solicitor, it's a good idea to prepare a short 'heads of agreement' (i.e. a brief summary) summarising your intentions, as shown in Appendix 8.

Limited company

Should I form a limited company?

This is not usually a good idea to start off with.

As an alternative to the first two types you may decide to form a limited company. There is one main advantage in doing this, namely that your liability is limited to the share capital of the company. In other words, in theory, you personally cannot be made bankrupt for the actions of the

company. However, if you have given guarantees, or if you have not properly fulfilled your duties as a director, then you certainly can be made to pay for the company's debts.

If what you are going to start is only a small concern, I don't think that you should consider a limited company initially due to the burdensome administration involved. If your business grows, however, then there may be tax, and other, advantages from incorporation so it may be advantageous.

Lawpack has published a *Limited Company Kit*, which should give you all the help you need in this area and I suggest that if this subject is of interest to you, you acquire this particular publication.

Unincorporated association

A further structure is available where a group of individuals want to get together to form a club or organisation for some activity or other. They may consider forming an unincorporated association. Unless the business has aspirations to make a profit for its members, the surpluses will not be subject to a tax charge. However, if the organisation has spare cash which it invests or places on deposit so that it yields income, then that income will be taxed. The tax position of unincorporated associations should be agreed with the Inland Revenue at an early stage.

No specific action has to be taken in order to set up an unincorporated association, but the association should hold formal meetings and keep proper records of the proceedings in order to protect members.

For the purpose of this book, the assumption has been made that the business is a sole proprietor although the majority of the sections are common to all structures.

Who you need to tell and where to find advice

A chartered accountant

He will be the main friend you'll have while you are in business, as not only will he help you prepare accounts and tax returns, but also he will be abreast of your business affairs. He will therefore be knowledgeable about your business and will be a good source of confidential advice and information at times of decision making. Include him and confide in him from the start (if you cannot trust your present accountant, then find one you can!) and he will be worth his fees.

Your solicitor

The main point to learn in connection with getting the most from your solicitor (or any of your professional advisers) is that if you keep him well informed, he will be better able to give advice. So, before you start up in business, it's a good idea to drop him a line telling him of your major new venture.

Your bank

Very few businesses operate without using a bank account, so I strongly urge that you open an account if you don't have one already.

Whether you keep two accounts, one for your business and one for private use, is up to you. If you maintain one account only to be used for

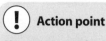

Action point

Have you opened your business account yet?

both purposes, your accountant will naturally see all the private expenditure which goes through it. You may not want him to be privy to all your private financial affairs. If you keep two accounts, then this problem doesn't arise, but there is a separate problem – namely you must be very careful to process all your business payments through the business account. If you pay for the odd business bill through your private account, then unless you tell your accountant about it, he will never pick it up and your accounts and VAT returns will be inaccurate (see Chapter 2 for further information).

On the whole, it is recommended that all sole traders operate a separate business account. Having opened a business account and kept your bank manager abreast of your business performance, he will be the most sympathetic ear to talk to if extra finance is required.

A mortgage lender

It is possible that your mortgage lender may prevent you from working from home. This is more likely if you develop a business that radically affects the approach to, the look of or use of your home. Indeed, if what you do increases the risk of damage to your home, such as a greater risk of fire, this may also impinge on the mortgage agreement. So, check all the legal documents relating to the mortgage and, if in any doubt, contact the lender for his ruling.

An insurance adviser

You will be subject to all sorts of new insurance problems once you are in business (e.g. public liability, product liability, employer's liability) and a good many others. In addition, you may wish to take advantage of the

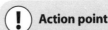

(!) Action point

Have you contacted your insurance adviser to make sure that you have the necessary insurance cover for what you want to do?

opportunity you will have of taking out a self-employed pension plan. It is as well to call in your insurance or financial services adviser at an early stage to make sure that you are properly covered for all the new insurable liabilities.

So, inform your current insurers that you are running a business from home. While you may already have sufficient cover for the house, its contents, public liability, you may need to extend the cover for:

- business equipment

- hazardous materials

- goods in transit

- employer's liability (if you have employees)

- money held on the premises

- product liability or other indemnity insurance

- extra public liability

- extra motor insurance for business use of vehicles, especially if others drive your vehicle while helping you in your business

- business interruption

- key man insurance (i.e. the insurance of a worker without whom the business would be at serious risk)

- credit card

- income protection

- private medical insurance

as well as:

- taking out an appropriate pension policy

Remember to notify your insurers in advance of working from home, as you may risk invalidating your household insurance policy.

As you work from home, your insurers may require an additional premium on your current insurance and they may ask you to make changes to your home for safety reasons.

Your landlord

The same comments that apply to a mortgage lender also apply to your landlord. You should check your lease for any conditions relating to business use.

The media

Contact your local radio station, newspapers, TV and magazines, as well as anyone else who may help you promote your business. But do remember that wonderful ditty:

 Action point

Have you prepared a simple strategy for working with the local paper to get publicity for your business?

He who whispers down a well
About the goods he has to sell
Never makes as many dollars
As he who climbs a tree and hollers.

A marketing, website and design consultant

Consider marketing, presentation and selling. Your business's name, premises, website and stationery all affect what your potential customers think of you. This is

 Action point

Have you planned your website yet?

not a legal requirement, more about how to succeed.

Business Link

This organisation, an agency of the Department of Trade and Industry, provide general information and advice free of charge to anyone setting up in business, and if they don't know the answer to a particular problem, they will know who to refer it to. For example, you may want to know what sort of grants are available for your particular venture and Business Link are more than likely to have the answer on whom to contact, at its fingertips. Call its helpline on 0845 600 9006 or visit www.businesslink.gov.uk.

The NFEA

The National Federation of Enterprise Agencies (NFEA) are a network of independent local enterprise agencies who provide a range of services, including a counselling service, for small businesses. They give analysis and advice concerning individual problems. If such help is needed, you can refer your problem in detail to them for their expert advice and the service is free of charge. To find your nearest LEA, visit www.nfea.co.uk.

CHAPTER 2
Tax and accounting

Part-time working from home

If what you are going to be doing is simply making some sundry earnings on top of what you do already, then, perhaps, most of the contents of this book will not apply to you. However, you will need to check through the action points and in particular:

 Action point

Have you informed the Inland Revenue of the existence of your business?

- tell the Inland Revenue what you are up to (see page 31);

- send it accounts by filling in the appropriate boxes on your tax return in line with the prescribed layout – see Appendix 7.

Self-employed or employed?

Before we get going, you need to sort out a very important question first of all: are you sure that you are self-employed? You must get this sorted out at the outset, particularly for your employer (if that is what he is) because he could be landed with a huge tax bill if he gets it wrong. If in doubt, get professional advice and, if still in doubt, ask for a ruling from your tax office.

Working from Home

The Inland Revenue is keen to classify self-employed people as employees because of the greater National Insurance contribution (both the employer and the employee pay it) and higher Income Tax payable. Employees don't have many expenses they can claim against tax (see page 67) and both they and their

? 'Employed' or 'self-employed', it's pretty black-and-white isn't it?

No, there are grey areas. Go through the questionnaire; if in doubt, get legal advice.

employers pay National Insurance on their wages, etc. On the other hand, not only do the self-employed have a much greater range of allowable expenses (see page 34) as they can claim against their profits, but their total National Insurance contributions tend to be much lower.

Answering the following questions should help you judge whether you are self-employed or not. **Note:** There are separate and new rules for workers in the construction industry; the following questions are not appropriate for such workers.

1. Is there a contract of service, i.e. a contract of employment?

   A 'no' answer indicates self-employment.

2. Is there a contract for services, i.e. a notice supplied by the person carrying out the work (A), indicating the nature of goods or services he will provide to B (this need not be written)?

   A 'yes' answer indicates self-employment.

3. Is the person who does the work in business on his own account?

   A 'yes' answer indicates self-employment.

4. If the person is in business on his own account, has evidence been provided that this is indeed the case (e.g. copy accounts, the payment of Class 2 National Insurance contributions)?

   A 'yes' answer indicates self-employment.

5. Are the hours worked decided by the person doing the work?

   A 'yes' answer indicates self-employment.

6. Are the days worked decided by the person doing the work?

   A 'yes' answer indicates self-employment.

7. Does the person doing the work decide when to take his own holidays?

   A 'yes' answer indicates self-employment.

8. Does the business proprietor supervise the work?

   A 'no' answer indicates self-employment.

9. Is the person part-and-parcel of the business?

   A 'no' answer indicates self-employment.

10. Does the person supply tools and/or materials when he carries out the work?

    A 'yes' answer indicates self-employment.

11. Does the person doing the work give the business an invoice for the work done?

    A 'yes' answer indicates self-employment.

12. Does the business calculate how much to pay the person doing the work and give a payslip?

    A 'no' answer indicates self-employment.

13. Is self-employment the intention of both parties?

    A 'yes' answer indicates self-employment.

14. Is the person bound by the customer care 'credo' (i.e. philosophy) of the business?

    A 'no' answer indicates self-employment.

15. Is the person carrying out the work required to wear a uniform or dress tidily at the diktat of the business?

    A 'no' answer indicates self-employment.

16. Is the person carrying out the work provided with a car or transport by the business?

   A 'no' answer indicates self-employment.

17. In the event of sickness, does the business continue to pay the person while not at work?

   A 'no' answer indicates self-employment.

18. Is the person carrying out the work at liberty to work for other businesses?

   A 'yes' answer indicates self-employment.

19. Is the person carrying out the work required to work in order to perform a specific task?

   A 'yes' answer indicates self-employment.

20. Does the business, on asking this person to carry out work for it, assume any responsibility or liability characteristic of an employment, such as employment protection, employees' liability, pension entitlements, etc.?

   A 'no' answer indicates self-employment.

21. Is the person who does the work paid an agreed price per job?

   A 'yes' answer indicates self-employment (i.e. he is not paid for the hours he works but for the work carried out).

22. Is the work carried out regularly?

   A 'no' answer indicates self-employment.

23. Does the individual work for other people?

   A 'yes' answer indicates self-employment.

24. Does the person carrying out the work advertise?

   A 'yes' answer indicates self-employment.

25. Does the person carrying out the work have headed stationery?

   A 'yes' answer indicates self-employment.

26. Can the person send a substitute? If so, has this ever happened?

A 'yes' answer indicates self-employment.

27. Does the person have to rectify faulty workmanship in his own time and at his own expense?

A 'yes' answer indicates self-employment.

Once you have addressed these questions, you should now begin to know whether you are self-employed. However, if the Inland Revenue disagrees, a definite answer can only be given by the courts.

Value Added Tax

Value Added Tax (VAT) is a tax with its own set of complicated rules and I cannot hope to give you a detailed introduction in a book of this size. However, the basics you need to know are that, unless you run a business with a turnover of more than £60,000 (2005/06 figure) and

> **? When must I start adding VAT onto my invoices?**
>
> *For most businesses, when your turnover exceeds £60,000 a year (2005/06 figure).*

the product or service attracts VAT (and most of them do), you probably don't need to register for VAT. Most people working from home are not registered because they don't have to be registered. But if you would like to register *voluntarily* (to claim VAT back on your expenses, etc.), you should contact the nearest VAT office for the registration forms.

If you register for VAT, you will gain from one immediate benefit and possibly suffer from one immediate disadvantage. In addition to this disadvantage, you must also realise that being registered for VAT involves certain legal responsibilities.

So, before an explanation of the pros and cons of voluntary registration, you have to ask yourself the following question:

Working from Home

'Am I prepared to take on the responsibility of writing up my accounting records in accordance with certain legal standards, and doing so every quarter?'. If you are the sort of person who finds administration, filing and bookwork a chore, you probably should not voluntarily register for VAT as it will become an extra problem for you.

However, you could avoid this extra problem by employing an accountant to prepare the VAT returns, but this will cost extra money.

If you are unsure about the answer to this question, it should be emphasised that there are many thousands of VAT-registered traders and, when you consider that many are small business people with no training in book-keeping, it should become apparent that keeping proper VAT records is not an insuperable task. If you are prepared to learn the simple VAT accounting rules and stick to them, you should certainly consider registering for VAT.

 Action point

If you have decided to register for VAT, or if you are going to have to register, have you done so?

If your turnover is to be above the annual VAT threshold from the start (£60,000 is the 2005/06 figure), then you have no choice in the matter. Registration is compulsory in your case. If your turnover (sales) has exceeded the threshold, for whatever reason, and you have failed to register, this could have expensive consequences and you are firmly advised to seek professional advice as soon as possible.

What is the benefit of registering? It is, as we say, so that you can reclaim VAT on most business purchases. If you are not registered, then no reclaim can be made.

What is the possible disadvantage? The possible disadvantage is that you have to add VAT to all your VATable sales. This means that all such sales are automatically more expensive than they would be if you were not registered. This may put you at a disadvantage against your competitors if they are not registered for VAT. However, if your customers themselves are registered for VAT (i.e. if you are dealing with other businesses rather than the public), the chances are that they will in turn be able to reclaim any VAT that you charge and so this would not disadvantage your business.

If you feel that you are prepared to treat VAT registration with the due respect that it requires, and that your sales will not suffer unduly as a result, then you should consider registering.

The changes you will need to make in the day-to-day running of your business are as follows:

1. For sales, you will need to issue VAT invoices and you will have to record the amount of VAT you charge (called 'output tax').

2. For purchases, you will have to keep a VAT invoice for all your purchases in order to be able to reclaim VAT and you will have to record the amount of VAT you have paid (called 'input tax').

Two final points on this introduction to VAT:

1. If your business is one that will attract a regular refund of VAT, you will be offered the chance of receiving your repayment monthly and not quarterly. Unless the sums are considerable (i.e. more than £500 a month), you are advised to resist monthly VAT returns because attending to them monthly rather than quarterly can become a nuisance.

2. You may apply to fill in just one annual VAT return and pay your VAT over nine months with a balancing payment at the end.

How to register for VAT

Telephone your nearest VAT office (under 'Customs and Excise' in the telephone book) to arrange for a VAT registration application form to be sent to you and to be registered for 'Cash Accounting', so that you only have to complete one VAT return a year.

Working from Home

National Insurance

Along with Income Tax, if you are going self-employed, you will almost certainly have to register for National Insurance.

What this means is that, unless your profits are going to be below the prescribed limit (this figure, which is changed every year by the Chancellor of the Exchequer, is included in Appendix 1), you will have to pay Class 2 contributions. If your profits are to be above a

 How do I register for self-employed National Insurance contributions?

Contact your local NI office, listed in the phone book.

further threshold (again see Appendix 1 for this figure), you will have to pay Class 4 contributions as well.

Class 2 contributions can be collected each month by direct debit, and you probably have attended to this obligation already when you filled in the forms (mentioned on page 31) to advise the Inland Revenue that you are now self-employed.

Class 4 contributions, if you have to pay them, will be collected along with your Income Tax liabilities and, apart from the pain of parting with the money, is a simple matter of ensuring that your self-assessment tax return is filled in correctly (see page 31 for more information).

But we do need to return to Class 2 again. If your profits are going to be below the Class 2 threshold, you still need to inform the National Insurance authorities that you are self-

Action point

When registering your business with the taxman and the NI office, if your profits are going to be below the Class 2 threshold, have you claimed exception – so that you do not have to pay them?

employed, but, at the same time, you should claim exception from paying these particular contributions simply because your profits are below the threshold. It does seem a bit unnecessary registering to pay and then registering not to pay, but this is how it works.

You can apply for exception by applying for a 'certificate of low earnings exception'. You must apply for this as soon as possible because they can only be backdated for up to 13 weeks before the date of application. If you do apply for exception, you may lose entitlement to other benefits, so do take advice.

If you are self-employed in your spare time as an extra to your permanent job, unless you qualify for exception, you must also pay Class 2 contributions, even if you are also paying National Insurance as an employee. However, if your Class 1 payments exceed a certain threshold, you may be able to defer payment of your Class 2 contributions. Take advice from your local tax office.

> **?** **Is National Insurance payable if you are self-employed?**
>
> *Yes, unless your profits are below a certain level. You need to register either way.*

PAYE

Taking somebody on can be one of the early big milestones in any business. What follows can also apply to private individuals who are employing people such as cooks, nannies, gardeners, etc. and so, while most of what follows relates to the things that a business person should do, private individuals should be aware that they may well be caught by the PAYE regulations that relate to employing people.

There is no clear guidance one can give. Having said this, the only answer is that you have to obey the law, but knowing what the law is is not always easy in itself.

If you take on somebody and you are paying him more than £94 a week, no matter what his age, you have to pay National Insurance contributions and the rate is 12.8 per cent. If this is the case, then the first thing you should do is inform the Inland Revenue that you have taken somebody on and the

Working from Home

second thing you should do is decide how you are going to handle the PAYE payment obligations.

In my view, the simplest way of meeting your obligations is to ask a professional accountant to look after the PAYE side of things for you. He will tell you how much to pay your employees net of tax and National Insurance and he will also send you the appropriate PAYE slip for making the monthly or quarterly payments to the Inland Revenue. He will also be able to help you with the Annual Return (P35) and with the benefit forms (P11Ds).

A second alternative is to buy a simple computer program and do the work in-house yourself. These are good, economically priced and well worth the investment in both software and stationery.

A third alternative is to use the manual forms the Inland Revenue sends you. In my view, these are not easy forms to follow and are definitely a worse option than the first two suggestions above.

A fourth alternative is to go and buy a manual wages system from the local stationer. This would certainly be better than using the Inland Revenue forms but, in this computer-centred age, I certainly recommend options 1 and 2.

If you take on someone earning less than £94 per week, there will be no National Insurance contributions to worry about. However, you may still find that you need to deduct tax from your employee's earnings. This depends on the tax code you have been directed to use, which is either shown on the Form P45 from his previous job or advised by the Inland Revenue. If you take on someone who does not have a P45 (because he wasn't working

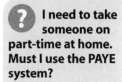

? I need to take someone on part-time at home. Must I use the PAYE system?

If he is employed by you, yes. If he remains self-employed, no. If in doubt, after completing the questionnaire on pages 20–23, take advice from the Inland Revenue.

previously or has an existing job which is to continue), he will need to complete a P46 and send it to the Revenue. The Revenue will then send you a notice of coding, which may well direct you to deduct tax if there are other earnings.

If you are unsure as to whether the person you are taking on is going to be treated as an employee or self-employed, then apply the test shown on pages 20–23.

If this test leaves you none the wiser, perhaps the best answer to give you is to go and discuss the matter with the Inland Revenue or with a professional accountant. Make no mistake, it is a complicated business and one that is very important to get right. Employers should not turn a blind eye to their obligations.

If you take on someone casually on both an infrequent and irregular (possibly one-off) basis, the Inland Revenue is very unlikely to be concerned about the matter. There is a very well-known legal maxim 'de minimis non curat lex', which means 'the law is not concerned with trifles'. The best advice I can give you is to say 'Is this a trifle?'. If it is, and you can justify it as being so to a visiting inspector, then regard the person as being casual – a trifle. If the matter has obviously some regularity and (shall we say) meaty content – in other words not a trifle – then I suggest that you go and talk it through with the Inland Revenue or an accountant and take the action that arises from such an approach.

What is PAYE?

PAYE stands for Pay As You Earn. It represents a logical system whereby week by week or month by month an employer deducts tax and National Insurance in such a way that, at the end of the income tax year, the right amount of tax and National Insurance has been deducted and handed over to the authorities. It works in the following way:

Let's say that you earn £15,000 a year and your personal tax-free allowance is £3,000. Let's also suppose that the rate of tax that you are paying is ten per cent (wouldn't that be nice?).

Working from Home

If you paid tax just once a year, you would calculate the tax as follows:

- £15,000 less your tax-free personal allowance £3,000 gives you...
- taxable pay £12,000 on which...
- tax at ten per cent is £1,200.

The way PAYE works is to collect that £1,200 on a monthly basis (£100 per month) and that works as follows:

The Inland Revenue issues tables that show the tax-free pay for each of the various PAYE codes for each week and for each month throughout the year. They also issue tax tables that tell

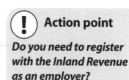

! Action point

Do you need to register with the Inland Revenue as an employer?

you how much tax to deduct from somebody's pay for each of the weeks and months throughout the year. I won't go into the details here (your eyes may be glazing over already by now), but if we take the case of somebody with a tax allowance of £3,000, that would equate to a PAYE code of 300. During the year, at whatever payment date you were making a wages or salary payment you would look up the appropriate amount of free pay for somebody with a tax code of 300 at that moment. What you would find is that if you were paying somebody £15,000 a year, each month you would pay him £1,250 gross. Of this sum, £250 is tax-free pay (you would find this in Table A of the documentation you are given by the Inland Revenue) so that you apply the tax rate of ten per cent (using Table B) to the £1,000 taxable pay. This means that you would deduct £100 from the pay each month and send that off to the Inland Revenue. At the end of the year you would have paid over £1,200.

However, you have to remember that, in addition to doing this tax calculation, you would also have to work out the National Insurance. It is quite a palaver and this is why I recommend using a computer or getting somebody else to do it.

Income Tax

If you are going to run your own business from home, then so far as the tax authorities are concerned, you have to tell them that you are going self-employed and you have to fill in forms CWF1 and CA5601. To get these forms, simply phone or call in at your local tax office or visit www.inlandrevenue.gov.uk. You must do this within three months of starting or they are liable to make you pay a penalty (or fine) of £100.

> **?** **How do I tell the Inland Revenue that I am self-employed?**
>
> *By completing and sending it forms CWF1 and CA5601, available online at www.inlandrevenue.gov.uk/menus/otherforms.htm.*

When to pay

The self-employed normally pay their tax in three annual instalments:

1. By 31 January – the amount is normally half of last year's tax bill.

2. By 31 July – the same amount as in 1.

3. By the next 31 January – the amount due is calculated on the actual income returned for the tax year less the payments you have already made (as above).

Self-assessment

If you are self-employed, either as a sole trader or in a partnership, you must complete a tax return annually. A tax return is used to work out how much tax and National Insurance contributions you have to pay. Instead of paying tax on your income, you pay tax on your business profits and like a company, you can deduct your business expenses from your income to work out how much taxable profit you have made.

Working from Home

Usually the Inland Revenue will send you a tax return automatically in April, but if it doesn't, it is still your responsibility to ask for one. If you want the Inland Revenue to work out your tax bill, you should fill in the return and send it in by 30 September, but if you are happy to calculate the tax yourself, the final deadline is 31 January. If you don't meet this deadline, you will be fined and may also be charged additional penalties.

It is always easier to complete your tax returns if all your paperwork is in order. If you are self-employed or a sole trader, legally you must keep records of your income (and any capital gains) for at least five years and ten months after the end of the tax year.

Most traders leave this matter to their accountants. If you are not going to use the services of an accountant, I suggest that you contact the local tax office in good time for its free advice on this aspect which it will give in connection with helping you complete your tax return. You can also contact the Inland Revenue's Self-Assessment Helpline on 0845 900 0444.

Business rates and Council Tax

It is possible that, if it knows you are conducting a business from home, the local authority will assess you to business rates. This will depend on what you propose doing and what the local planning laws say.

In principle, someone using part of his home as an office is unlikely to be of interest to his local authority. However, if you start manufacturing things and effectively change the use of part of your home, then, yes, it is going to come knocking.

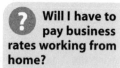

? Will I have to pay business rates working from home?

It depends on the space occupied by your business – contact your local authority for advice.

On the other hand, if you were to tell the local authority that you no longer use a bedroom as a bedroom but as an office, you may even get a reduction in the Council Tax payable. But it may undo this saving by slapping a business rate charge on the room.

Capital Gains Tax

If a specific part of your house is set aside for business purposes, then that proportion of your profits on the sale of the house will, in theory, be taxable. However, if you do not have any rooms used exclusively for business purposes, you normally will not be liable to any Capital Gains Tax (CGT) if you sell your house.

Having said this, I have never known the taxman to claim any CGT due to the fact that a small business had been run in a private residence which was subsequently sold.

The key word in this section is 'exclusively'. If, say, you have set aside a bedroom as an office, in my view, it is likely to be still regarded as a bedroom. However, if you used a room downstairs as an office and it had separate access for customers from the main house, it might attract interest and you should seek professional advice over the tax implications.

Inheritance Tax

Inheritance Tax (IHT), like VAT, is a tax with its own set of complicated rules. In many ways it is worse than VAT because the tax payable can quickly grow to a truly frightening figure. In the briefest terms, if you were to die leaving assets worth more than £275,000, the Chancellor of the Exchequer will want 40 per cent of the balance in tax. 40 per cent is a truly shocking rate of tax; it is the starting rate and it applies to just about everything you own at the time of your death.

With many houses now worth at least this sum, the Chancellor is currently reaping more from the taxpayer from IHT than he is getting from what we give him when we buy wines and spirits. You can see how this tax is no minnow that can be ignored. In other words, while this book is concerned with working from home and not with IHT saving, you may need to take professional advice about this matter.

Having said this, and trying to stress the importance of ensuring that your estate is as well protected as it can be from the ravages of IHT, it is unlikely that, having decided to work from home, you will suffer more IHT than otherwise may be the case.

I don't think it is at all likely that IHT will have any impact on anyone working from home, but, if you have any doubts, please seek professional advice.

Business expenses

If you are self-employed and working from home, which expenses are tax-deductible? The following is a guide:

Basic costs and use of home for work

Normally allowed: Proportion of telephone, lighting, heating, cleaning, insurance. Proportion of rent and Council Tax, if you use part of the home exclusively for business – claiming ground rent and Council Tax may mean some Capital Gains Tax to pay if you sell your home, but this is unlikely. Cost of goods bought for resale and raw materials used in business. Advertising, delivery charges, heating, lighting, cleaning, rates, telephone. Replacement of small tools and special clothing. Postage, stationery, relevant books and magazines. Accountant's fees. Bank charges on business accounts. Fees to professional bodies. Security expenditure.

> **? How do I estimate the proportion of relevant utility bills that I can offset against tax?**
>
> *Work out the area of your home taken up by your business; apply that as a percentage.*

Not allowed: Initial cost of machinery, vehicles, equipment, permanent advertising signs – but you can claim capital allowances. Cost of buildings. Providing for anticipated expenses in the future.

Note: You would normally ask an accountant to calculate and claim capital allowances. In principle, you are allowed to claim 25 per cent of most capital assets as a deduction against your profits, but it is quite complicated. Professional help is recommended.

Wages and salaries

Normally allowed: Wages, salaries, redundancy and leaving payments paid to employees. Pensions for past employees and their dependants. Staff training.

Not allowed: Your own wages or salary or that of any business partner. Your own drawings.

Tax and National Insurance

Normally allowed: Employer's National Insurance contributions for employees. Reasonable pay for your spouse, provided he or she is actually employed.

Not allowed: Income Tax. Capital Gains Tax. Inheritance Tax. Your own National Insurance contributions.

Entertaining

Normally allowed: Entertainment of own staff (e.g. Christmas party).

Not allowed: Any other business entertaining.

Pre-trading

Normally allowed: Revenue business expenditure (i.e. things you bought before you started to trade and are now being used in the business) incurred within five years before starting to trade.

Working from Home

Gifts

Normally allowed: Gifts costing up to £50 a year to each person so long as the gift advertises your business (or things it sells). Gifts (whatever their value) to employees.

Not allowed: Food, drink, tobacco or vouchers for goods given to anyone other than employees.

? How do I claim tax-deductible expenses?

By completing the relevant parts of a tax return.

Travelling

Normally allowed: Hotel and travelling expenses on business trips. Travel between different places of work. Running costs of own car; whole of cost if used wholly for business; proportion if used privately too.

Not allowed: Cost of buying a car or van, but you can claim capital allowances.

If a business leases a car costing more than £12,000, part of the leasing cost is disallowed for tax purposes. The rules are complicated, but, in principle, the more expensive the car you lease, the smaller the sum that you will be allowed to claim as a tax deduction in your accounts.

Interest payments

Normally allowed: Interest on overdrafts and loans for business purposes.

Not allowed: Interest on capital paid or credited to partners.

Hire purchase

Normally allowed: Hire charge part of instalments (i.e. the amount you pay less the cash price).

Not allowed: Cash price of what you are buying on hire purchase (but you may get capital allowances).

Hiring

Normally allowed: Reasonable charge for hire of capital goods, including cars.

Insurance

Normally allowed: Business insurance (e.g. employer's liability, fire and theft, motor, insuring employees' lives).

Not allowed: Your own life insurance.

Trade marks

Normally allowed: Fees paid to register a trade mark, design or patent.

Not allowed: Cost of buying a patent from someone else, but you may get capital allowances.

Legal costs

Normally allowed: Costs of recovering debts, defending business rights. Preparing service agreements. Appealing against rates, renewing a lease for a period not exceeding 50 years.

Not allowed: Expenses (including Stamp Duty) for acquiring land, buildings or leases. Fines and other penalties for breaking the law.

Repairs

Normally allowed: Normal repairs and maintenance to premises or equipment.

Not allowed: Cost of additions, alterations and improvements, but you may get capital allowances.

Debts

Normally allowed: Specific provisions for debts and debts written off.

Not allowed: General reserve for bad or doubtful debts.

Subscriptions

Normally allowed: Payments which secure benefits for your business or staff. Payments to societies that have arrangements with the Inland Revenue (in some cases only a proportion). But watch for possible National Insurance contributions.

Not allowed: Payments to political parties, churches, charities contributions (but small gifts to local churches and charities may be allowable).

Keeping accounts

Why prepare accounts?

1. Unless you are in business for enjoyment alone, you are obviously in business to make a profit. As a result, you will want to know how much profit or loss your business is making. This is exactly what a profit and loss account demonstrates and is probably the most important figure contained in the accounts. However, you will find other important information as well.

2. Accounts have to be prepared by law.

3. Accounts have to be prepared for the taxman.

Numbers 2 and 3 are negative reasons for preparing accounts (i.e. you only prepare accounts because you are compelled), so let us concentrate on the positive reason – namely that the documents are informative.

How to prepare them

As you may have seen in its advertisements, the Inland Revenue requires you to keep a record of everything you spend and receive. You can do this in a number of ways:

1. The simplest of methods
   For every item of money coming in and going out, you

keep a piece of paper (whether receipt, invoice or your own record), keeping incomings in a separate file (or maybe even in a separate 'pile') so that you, your accountant and eventually the Inland Revenue know the summary (or account) of what you have received and spent in your accounting year.

2. **A better way**

   In addition to the above, you actually write down what you have received and spent in a book. You can buy either a general stationery book, or a specialist accounting book (one

    Action point

   Have you bought a cash book yet? If so, have you headed up the columns in line with Appendix 7? Have you got some suitable files in which to keep your receipts, etc.?

   that shows you how to do it – this is usually on a weekly basis) or, and this is the best of the three, buy a cash analysis book and write the information in it. These books are multi-column (the more columns the better) and, once you have got used to them (they are extremely simple and one that my firm recommends over any other system), they are extremely useful as both a record of what you have done and a source of useful information of all that has gone on in your business.

   The left-hand side of the book records money coming in and the right, money going out. Appendix 7 provides a useful set of titles with which to head up each column.

3. **You can computerise**

   (a) The simplest and cheapest way to do this is to create a spreadsheet using the titles for each column as just described in point 2 above.

   (b) You can buy a ready-made computerised package, none of which I particularly like, but, on the other hand, lots of others do find them helpful, and so I shouldn't denigrate them.

(c) You could engage the services of an accountant who lets you keep your books online.

The last point I should make is that keeping accounts is like flower arranging: there are a great many different ways in which you can do it and there is no one way that is the right way. The way that is going to be best for you is the way you find that you like best; it is going to be up to you to find the way that you really like. So, why not ask a number of small business people to show you how they do it and pick the one that you understand best and like using best.

Understanding accounts

The profit and loss account

Essentially, this is a comparatively easy statement to understand. It lists the money that a business has received (or is due to receive) during the period covered by the accounts and, from them, deducts the money the business has paid out (or has been due to pay out) during the period (expenditure). The difference is the profit or loss.

If the statement is read slowly and carefully, there should be no problem in understanding it, especially if you remember exactly why it has been prepared – to show you how well or badly the business has done during the period covered by the accounts.

There are, however, two accounting expressions which may be a little difficult to understand. These are:

Stocks. In most businesses there are goods bought in one accounting period and sold in another. The cost of these goods should be charged, not against the profits of the period in which they were bought, but against the profits of the period in which they were sold. It is necessary to deduct the cost of any unsold stocks at the end of the period covered by the accounts, as this cost will be added to the relevant future accounting period.

Such stocks are called 'closing stocks' and if the accounts contain a figure of 'opening stocks', you will realise that this figure refers to unsold stocks at the end of the previous accounting period. (Check to see if this is so.)

Depreciation. In a business you own, plant machinery and/or equipment which will wear out in time. It is the accountant's estimate of how much this property of the business has worn out during the period covered by the accounts.

The balance sheet

As explained, the profit and loss account shows how much the business has made or lost during the period covered by the accounts. It is an 'account' or 'story'. The balance sheet shows how much, in theory, the business was worth at the end of the period covered by the accounts. It is a 'photograph' of the business at a particular date.

The balance sheet is divided into two parts – part 1, the statement of total net assets, shows the net total value of everything the business owns less everything it owes. If you think about this, you will see that such a total figure means, in theory, how much the business is worth.

Part 2, the statement of source of finance, shows how the assets listed in part 1 have been paid for.

Total net assets

As with the profit and loss account, read it through slowly, carefully bearing in mind the purpose of the statement. Again, there are certain accounting terms which may need further explanation:

Assets. The word asset is an omnibus term for anything the business owns.

Fixed assets. A fixed asset is something bought for the business for use in running the business (e.g. a factory or machine).

Current assets. A current asset is something paid for and for which is intended to turn into profit within the near future (e.g. stocks).

Depreciation. Depreciation is the amount by which the accountant has estimated the asset has worn out since it was first bought.

Stocks. As we have seen in the profit and loss account, stocks are bought with the intention of reselling them in one form or another at a later date. Thus any unsold stocks at an accounting period end form part of the current assets at that date.

Debtors. This is the money owed to a business by customers, etc.

Prepayments. These are usually payments made in advance. For example, an insurance premium may have been paid up to a date after the balance sheet date. The amount paid in advance is, theoretically, repayable by the insurance company and, as such, is like a debtor, but is called a prepayment.

Current liabilities. This refers to money which a business owes to other people.

Creditors. This is the most usual type of current liability and therefore refers to money owed by the business as at the balance sheet date.

Working capital. This is the total of current assets less current liabilities. It is a net total thrown up within the balance sheet and, in crude terms, if fixed assets form the engine which runs the business, working capital is the fuel of that engine.

The source of finance

We have established that part 1 of the balance sheet shows you how much a business is worth in theory. However, to round off the statement it must be shown how the net assets have been paid for (i.e. how they have been financed). The usual sources of finance are:

Proprietors' funds:

Capital introduced. This is the money that the owner of the business has 'put up' to start the business as well as any additional funds he may have contributed.

Profits. If the business has been making profits, the money thereby created will have paid for some of the assets. Profits are a source of finance.

Losses. If the business has been making losses, then money will have flowed out of the business – hence losses are a deduction from the proprietors' funds.

(As any profit or loss as shown in the balance sheet will have come from the profit and loss account, the two figures on the statements should be the same.)

Drawings. This is the money you have drawn from the business to live off.

Loans to the business:

If a bank or anyone else has lent money to the business, it is another source of finance.

CHAPTER 3

Rules and regulations

Health and safety

The ramifications of health and safety regulations stretch far and wide. Even if you are self-employed, working from home and with no employees, you are still affected by them. For the most part, these regulations are common sense because it has to be a good idea to work in a safe environment, both for your benefit and for those who live in the same building. Also, showing that your business has sound health and safety procedures may assist you in getting competitive insurance premiums.

To start with, if you are going to be handling materials, especially toxic or inflammable materials, then you must observe all the directions you have been given in the instructions and directions that come with the product, as well as any special training you have undergone.

However, in more general terms, the law requires you to protect the health, safety and welfare of others, whether they are employees or not. This may include visitors to your home, as well as other people in your household who may be affected.

 Action point

Have you conducted an appropriate health and safety assessment of your working environment?

Working from Home

The way in which you are expected to comply is to carry out a risk assessment and you do this, in effect, by:

- identifying any hazards (i.e. something that may cause you harm – you can find an elementary description of some common hazards in Appendix 9);

- deciding who may be harmed by them and how;

- assessing the risks (a risk is the chance, great or small, that someone will be harmed by a hazard) and taking appropriate action to remove the risks as far as possible;

- recording the findings of this assessment;

- setting up a procedure for checking these risks from time to time and taking any further steps that may be necessary.

In other words, if you are self-employed and working from home, you should review your environment to ensure that you have proper working arrangements with respect to, amongst others, the following:

- Lighting

- Heat

- Age of equipment

- Servicing of equipment

- Protective equipment and/or clothing

- Safety of power supply

- Posture when seated

- Taking sufficient breaks

- First aid provision

If you have five employees or more, you must also draw up a health and safety policy. For more information on what to include, as well as advice on any aspect of health and safety, contact the Health and Safety Executive (tel. 0870 154 5500, www.hse.gov.uk).

Environmental health

If you are setting up an office or shop, or running a food/catering business (whether from home or not), you should contact your

Action point

Do you need to inform the Environmental Health Services of your local council?

local authority. There are certain standards of health and safety that apply to this sort of employment and the local environmental health department will advise you appropriately.

Food Standards is a minefield, but, in principle for the purposes of this book, there are two things to remember about selling food or food products:

- There should always be adequate facilities for the preparation and serving of food.

- Food handling procedures should be such that you take all appropriate measures to avoid food being exposed to the risk of contamination.

You may need to take advice from the Environmental Health Services of your local council or visit www.foodstandards. gov.uk.

Planning permission

You may need to apply for planning permission from your local council if your home-based occupation changes the use of a building. The general rule is that if you are using less than half your home as office space, you don't need to apply for planning permission, but if what you do is noisy or somehow adversely affects your neighbours (e.g. your activity creates pollution or makes parking difficult for them), then no matter how small the business is, you will almost certainly need permission to carry it out.

Licences

If you are planning to be in the retail business, the consumer protection authorities have further regulations that you must comply with. Licences are needed for alcohol sale, market traders, pet shops, food shops, restaurants (both static and mobile) and cosmetics businesses. Apply to your local authority environmental health department.

> **? Do I need a licence to run a food business from home?**
>
> *You must register with your local authority environmental health department at least 28 days before opening.*

Trading Standards

If you are selling goods, as opposed to services, your local Trading Standards Office should be able to offer free advice on how you should sell your products. It has a wealth of literature on the rules, particularly for labelling, safety requirements and trade descriptions. Guidance is also available on www.tradingstandards.gov.uk.

Trading Standards can also help with advice on the regulations governing your relationship with your customers and whether your terms of business are fair.

Data protection

Under data protection law, if you keep any personal information on other people, you have to register with the Information Commissioner and explain how you are going to use the information. This law also gives private individuals the right to see what you are

> **? I keep customer details on card files only. Do I need to register under the Data Protection Act?**
>
> *No, but you still need to apply the principles of the Act.*

holding and to check its accuracy. The Commissioner can be contacted through www.informationcommissioner.gov.uk.

The Business Names Act 1985

Whether this applies to you will depend on what name you decide to trade under. If you are not going to trade under your own name, then you should know that the above Act, which applies to all businesses not trading under the proprietor's own name, states that:

'Any person (who is trading under a business name which is not his own name) shall:

(a) State in legible characters on all business letters, written orders for goods or services, invoices, receipts and written demands for payments:

    i.   in the case of a partnership, the name of each partner;

    ii. in the case of an individual, his name;

    iii. in the case of a company, its corporate name; and

    iv. an address within Great Britain at which [the] service of any document relating to the business will be effective.

(b) In any premises where business is carried on, display in a prominent position so that it may easily be read by such customers or suppliers, a notice containing such name[s] and address[es].'

If you are a sole trader or in a partnership and you decide to use a business name, bear in mind the rules that the name must *not*:

- be offensive;

- include the words limited, plc, etc.;

- contain sensitive words and expressions (e.g. British, Authority, Architect – contact Companies House for advice; tel. 0870 333 3636).

Working from Home

Before deciding upon a name, do check that no one else is already using it. It may not be a problem if a sole trader is using it in another part of the country, but it could be an issue if someone is using it locally. You can do this by checking on the internet, as well as by visiting Companies House's website (www. companies-house.gov.uk), who can tell you if it has already been registered by a company and through the Patent Office's website (www.patent.gov.uk), who can tell you whether it is similar to a word or expression that has been registered as a trade mark.

> **? I don't intend to trade under my own name. What must I do?**
>
> *Prepare a notice and display it where any customers, visitors, etc. can see it.*

The Sale of Goods Act 1979

When you advertise your products or services (flyer, brochure, shop window, price list), you are inviting your customers to buy. If they accept your price, a contract is made when payment is made; at this point you (and your customer) have made a legal commitment. Except with 'distance selling' (on the internet or digital TV, by mail order, phone and fax, where there is a 'cooling-off' period), this contracted commitment cannot be cancelled without the agreement of both parties.

It is important that all claims you make when selling your goods/services are true. If they are not and the buyer can prove that his decision was based on these claims, there could be a claim against you.

In principle, goods that are sold must:

* be of satisfactory quality;
* be reasonably fit for any purpose made known to the seller;
* correspond with any advertising description.

On the other hand, services must be supplied:

- with care;

- with expected skill;

- on time; and

- at a charge that is seen to be fair.

If the seller/supplier fails in any of the above, the customer has a right in law to claim a refund or compensation. In addition, the seller/supplier cannot avoid liability to such a claim unless the defence meets a test of reasonableness.

While dealing with this topic, and bearing in mind that the Sale of Goods Acts, etc. protect the consumer, it is a good idea to tell prospective customers that you guarantee the quality, the care, the time for delivery, etc. of your products and services. Most businesses fail to mention this and, as a result, almost imply that the buyer is at risk if he decides to buy from them.

In contrast, those businesses that are upfront about how they guarantee to look after the customer in the above-mentioned areas (which they are legally obliged to be in any event) tend to stand out from their competitors by openly appearing to offer more than the others do, and therefore tend to sell more than their competitors.

There are a lot of rules and regulations that you need to be aware of and it is recommended that you read *A Trader's Guide to the Civil Law*, relating to the sale and supply of goods and services, available from your local Trading Standards Office. Also, a copy of the *Unfair Standard Terms* is available from the Office of Fair Trading, which offers lots of useful advice (tel. 0870 606 0321; www.oft.gov.uk).

Employment law

If you are going to employ people yourself, there is a whole raft of things to be aware of. I suspect that most people reading this book will not be employing anyone, but for those who do, here are the basic points to remember:

Working from Home

Employment contract

As soon as someone accepts your job offer, a contract of employment has been made, whether it is oral, written or implied.

Agree at the outset what the terms of employment should be and write them down. It is extraordinary how few employers, in spite of what the law says, issue a contract. It is very important to do this and I include in Appendix 6 a list of matters that should be included in such a document. Do use this as a starting point if it helps.

Even if you do not issue your potential employee with a contract, legally you still must give him a written statement of his employment particulars within two months of him commencing the job. This statement is not a contract, but it will count as evidence if there is a dispute in the future.

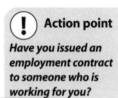

Action point

Have you issued an employment contract to someone who is working for you?

For further information, Lawpack publishes an *Employment Contracts Kit*, which includes a contract template.

Working hours

The Working Time Regulations came into force on 1 October 1998. Implementing a hefty chunk of the EU Social Chapter, they make big changes to the regulation of working hours, but have received remarkably little publicity.

The rules cover all workers, full-time and part-time, regardless of the size of firm for which they work, and they cover domestic staff. They extend to quite a few who, for tax purposes, would be counted as self-employed, such as freelancers.

The regulations provide that:

1. workers do not work more than 48 hours a week;

2. night workers do not work more than eight hours a night and are offered regular health assessments;

3. workers have a rest period of 11 consecutive hours between each working day;

4. workers have an in-work rest break of 20 minutes when working more than six hours;

5. workers have at least four weeks' paid leave each year.

Only in the case of the 48-hour week may individual workers choose to agree to ignore the regulations and work more than 48 hours. If they do, the agreement must be in writing and must allow the worker to bring the agreement to an end.

There is a number of other flexibilities and a lot of detailed definitions. If you would like to learn more, you can obtain a free copy of the DTI's *Guide to Working Time Regulations*, by calling 0845 600 0925.

Holiday pay

Holiday pay is normally dealt with in a contract of employment. By law, as an employer, you are obliged to let your employee take four weeks' annual leave. Part-time and casual employees are entitled to the same holidays as full-time employees, calculated pro rata.

Whether holiday pay is paid under a contract or under any other arrangement, it forms part of gross pay and is treated exactly the same as any other pay.

Minimum wage

See Appendix 3 for the minimum wage rates you must pay your employee(s). Employees who live and work as part of a family (e.g. nannies) are not entitled to the minimum wage.

For further information on these above-mentioned issues, as well as details on the other ever-changing regulations, such as maternity pay and redundancy, please refer to Lawpack's book entitled *Do-It-Yourself Employment Law*.

CHAPTER 4

You and your customers

Your office

This is probably not for me to tell you, particularly as I don't know what you will be doing! However, there are a whole lot of issues that you may like to consider, such as:

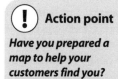

Action point

Have you prepared a map to help your customers find you?

- Do you need to set aside one room for your business?

- Does it need to be locked when you are not working?

- Has it got phone, fax and email/internet sockets?

- Do you need a separate business line or will answering the phone in the hall or kitchen be acceptable?

- If it is not to be conducted in a room set aside exclusively for business purposes, does it matter that the children may get at your records, products, cash tin, etc.?

One of the main problems you will find if you are running a self-employed business that is based at home is that this very fact tends to make the business look more of a hobby than a serious business.

If your customers have to step over the clutter of gumboots and children's tricycles and hear homely noises like the TV or radio blasting out pop music or children ragging as they arrive, and if the loo is a jumble of washing and wet towels, they will spot how very different your place of business is from one based in a shop, factory or office. This homely introduction can seriously detract from the appearance of your business, from the way your customer regards you and, indeed, from the price you can charge.

In my opinion, the key to solving this problem is understanding what your customers would like to see. What I mean is that the homebase can, if properly handled, be turned very much to your advantage.

The secret appears to be twofold:

1. You must keep the entrance tidy, clean and well maintained. You must give a good appearance for your customers as they approach and as they step inside. If you present a mess, they will not like it and, indeed, this may make them apprehensive about dealing with you from the start. If, on the other hand, the approach to, and visible welcome once inside, your house is pleasing, they will actually feel more relaxed than if they were visiting an office or shop. Formal business premises can, by their very nature, be intimidating (sometimes very intimidating, with the business owners blissfully unaware that this is the appearance their business gives) so that a friendly welcoming home can make people far more relaxed than otherwise.

2. Try to build on the warm, friendly efficient welcome by offering them the things that a shop or office can't. Chat to them about this or that, offer them a drink (hot, cold or alcoholic) and show them around your office, home, garden, workshop, go for a walk in the park, etc. You could even explain how it is that you work from home, etc. In short, treat them as a house guest (unless they react against

 Action point

Is the approach to your premises likely to impress your customers? If in doubt, ask a friend to visit pretending to be a potential customer and make him tell you what he sees.

this friendly sort of approach) and they are likely to become repeat customers simply because of the great rapport they feel has been established between you and them.

Your image

When starting your own business it is important to think of what image you want to portray to your customers through the design of your letterhead and the look of your website. It always helps if both these elements relate to each other visually.

Stationery

If you are printing business stationery, remember that it takes a little time to produce (for a start, it must look professional). It is best to decide what you need before you start to trade. If you want to generate all your stationery on your own computer, ensure it is properly designed first.

The sort of stationery you should order is:

- *Business letterhead.* This should give your trading name, address, telephone and fax number, website and email address, VAT registration number (if applicable) and the names of the proprietor(s) should also be included, unless they are exactly the same as the trading name. You could also include on the letterheading a very brief description of the sort of goods and services you provide.

- *Invoices/bills.* If you are registering for VAT, you are legally bound to include your VAT registration number on your invoices. Consequently, unless you are going to use a computerised invoicing system, you are advised to get invoices properly printed with a top and at least two copies. One copy will be filed in chronological or numerical order, so that you have an ascending record of every invoice you have issued. The other copy should be filed with all the other copy invoices you have issued to that customer, so you have a hard copy record of every sale you have invoiced to him. Some people get a third copy printed and file it with the unpaid copies, until it has been paid, and then file it with the copies of the paid invoices. Ask your printer to number them consecutively and put them into either pad or book form. The fact that they are numbered means that there is much less danger that you will lose one as they will all be padded up in numerical order.

However, if you are not registering for VAT, you are still advised to get invoices printed along the lines of the specimen in Appendix 7, less, of course, the VAT details. The reasons for getting invoices properly printed are:

1. They provide a much-needed and efficient basis for your sales records; if you only keep details on scraps of paper you are likely to get into a muddle.

2. A printed invoice is a much better advertisement than a page torn out of a duplicate book. If your customers see a well-designed and properly laid out invoice, they are more likely to respect your business efficiency than if all the details are handwritten.

If you are going to run a shop or restaurant with a till that produces till rolls, with all the necessary totals and VAT details, there will be no need to get invoices printed. However, only VAT-registered traders may show VAT details on any till rolls they issue.

- *Statements.* Whether or not you get statements printed depends on how many customers you sell to on credit. If you send one or two people an invoice in the post, to be paid at a later date, and one or more of them don't pay up, then you could easily send them one of your normal letterheadings with the statement details printed on it. However, if you are regularly sending out statements to a number of your customers, you should seriously consider having printed statements and possibly a computerised sales ledger. As with invoices, if your statements are printed and well laid out, it will be readily apparent to a reluctant debtor that you mean business, and expect to be paid.

- *Remittance advices*. When you pay your bills you do not (or should not) send off the cheque accompanied by the supplier's invoice (remember, you keep the invoice). Normally, you will be paying on an invoice, or on a statement, and will wish to keep the relevant documents for VAT and other purposes. Therefore, you should either send your cheque with a business card or compliment slip, writing the reference numbers, etc. on it so that the recipient can trace the payment or else you should prepare some remittance advices for your business.

- *Compliment slips/business cards/brochures*. These are always useful for a variety of purposes and are thoroughly recommended. They ought to be properly designed and give the essential information shown in the letterheading.

You may feel that your home business is so small that no printed stationery is required. If this is so, then you are strongly advised to record your sales in a duplicate book: your customer gets one copy and you keep the other.

The website

Once you have decided upon a business name, try to use it as your website address too, if possible. Before registering the address, you will have to check if it is available. If you want your address to end with co.uk, you can check its availability on the Nominet website (www.nic.uk), which looks after internet addresses in the UK. Your internet service provider can register it for you, but usually there is a small fee.

If you want your website to get bigger exposure on the web, you can register your site with the bigger search engines, such as Google, Yahoo and Altavista. Many of these companies will allow you to register yourself; go to their websites for further instruction.

Your time

While your customers may well determine what hours they expect you to be there, to a great extent you will be able to decide when you work, when to sit in the garden, when to get up in the morning, when to walk the dog, when to do the shopping and ironing, without having to get permission. (Yes, working from home does have its advantages!)

Taking holiday and time off

There are two particular problems, however, with working at home and they are closely related:

The first is that, in my experience, it is impossible to have a holiday at home if that is where your business is. You can never say 'I'm going to put my feet up and ignore callers today' or, if you do, your customers will soon take their business to someone else.

The second is that if the whole business depends on you and you alone, if you go on holiday, either the business will stop and this will cheese your customers off or you will have all calls directed to your mobile phone and the interruptions your business makes to your holiday will cheese your family and friends off.

The solutions to these problems are the same. Before I come to it, maybe I should accept that some people are so engaged in their work that the problems I've just described are not problems for them. However, even if this is the case, they should be aware that a business that dominates both home and family holidays could well be a problem, and a serious problem, for the other people living in the house. So, do be aware that if you become so engrossed in and fulfilled by your work at home, it may not be so wonderful for your nearest and dearest who would love to get you and their home to themselves for a while, but find that they never can. If you fall into this category, you may find the following thoughts helpful.

If you work at home, try to build in the following elements.

- Write down your terms of doing business, get it agreed by your nearest and dearest and give it to all your customers so that they know the deal as well.

- Have set hours for work and stick to them.

- Have a room that is set aside for work – a place you can lock up when you finish and say 'that's it for the day'.

- Have a separate phone line for the business with its own answering service.

- Try not to work all hours God gives you. You may like to take a leaf out of my book: I personally resolved some years ago not to work in my office on a Friday and this gives me a far better balance to my life than working five days and only having Saturdays and Sundays in which to squeeze all the other things in life one has to do. I started by telling everyone it would be an experiment that would last for three months – so, if it didn't work and if people got really fed up with me not being available on a Friday, I could retreat back to the five full days saying that the experiment didn't work out. After three months, it was working so well I had no intention at all of retreating. In fact, my clients were rather impressed by this development. 'What a good idea!' they would say and instantly took on board and willingly accepted this feature of how I did business. My employees also benefited. At least there was one day the boss was not going to be bothering them! And, as I have implied, I gained a balance in my life that I had not had before.

- Try to employ someone at an early stage, even part-time, to help you run the business. If he is good, he will be able to give you and your family freedom from feeling that you always have to 'be there'.

- When on holiday, let those who are affected by your departure (whether clients or employees) know where you are (in case of emergency), but do not call in each day to see how things are going. As someone once said, 'It's usually going far better when you are not there.'. Trust your people to run the business and prove that trust by letting them do it while you are on holiday.

Your customer relations

When dealing with customers it is essential to be businesslike. One key point of this is to be totally upfront with your customers by letting them know at the outset:

- what your service or product is going to cost;

- when you expect to be paid; and

- the ways they can pay you.

There is a tendency for people who go into business to be shy about asking for money and embarrassed that they might want to charge in the first place. Please try to avoid this approach at all costs because it seriously damages your credibility.

The key thing is for you to know what you are going to charge (having a price list that you can give away at first meeting is the best way of clearing this matter up) and then telling the customer at a very early stage when you expect to be paid.

 Action point

Have you prepared a price list? Have you established what you want your payment terms to be?

Over this last matter, I strongly recommend that you ask for the money upfront. And, if this makes you wobble and say 'How can I possibly take any money off my customer when he hasn't had anything from me yet?', just remember when you paid for this book. You probably bought it online and your credit card was debited, even though the book was delivered to you approximately two days later. If you paid for it in a store, then you will have paid for it at the checkout. Either way, you paid for it long before you gained any benefit from it. Just think about it – everything you buy is paid for upfront.

You should ensure that you too are paid the same way or, if your customer wants to pay in easy stages and not quite all of it upfront, you can always offer credit card facilities or ask for, for example, three cheques with two being post-dated for the next two months.

Guarantees

Guarantees are very important. If you don't offer your customers a guarantee, why should they buy from you? So, it is vital to offer something like a 'no quibble money-back guarantee' or a 'free-trial period of 30 days'.

As you sell your products you must reassure your customers that if they buy from you, they are guaranteed to get value for money. Tell them how the guarantee works and say that if things don't work out, you expect to be told and will do all in your power to rectify any problem.

 Action point

Have you established what your guarantees are to be? Do your customers know, at the outset, what your guarantees are?

Complaints

Mistakes that your own business makes are some of your greatest marketing tools. Such mistakes handled badly can lead to the loss of an awful lot of business. Handled well and you can create a really happy customer.

To regard your business mistakes as a marketing tool may sound paradoxical, but it is true. You should not dread a complaint, but see it as a means for taking the business forward and making it stronger.

This is because if you can repair a complaint in a way that makes your customer go 'wow', the customer will not only remain a customer, but will tell others how splendidly you resolved the problem to his benefit. Such referrals are not to be ignored.

Deal promptly and caringly with your business mistakes and own up to the complainant, admitting that he is right (that you goofed) and that you will do your utmost to put the matter not just right, but so right that the complainant feels that, if anything, you have gone overboard in rectifying the problem. If you do your utmost to repair the damage, you are likely to find that the complainant not just remains a customer, but becomes a truly loyal one.

CHAPTER 5

The employed at home

Even though it was a rare occurrence a few years ago, working from home is predicted to increase substantially in the next few years. This is partly due to the ever-expanding utilisation of modern technology and partly because more and more people are determining their own lifestyles and opting for the flexibility that working from home affords them.

It is generally accepted that homeworkers have the same rights as their colleagues working in the office. However, there are various issues that need to be addressed, and these are detailed below.

The employment contract

So far as homeworkers are concerned, the agreement should cover the following aspects:

- Working from home should be voluntary.

- Employment rights, including holiday entitlement, should not be affected because some or all of the work is carried out at home.

- Employment opportunities should not be affected because some or all of the work is carried out at home.

- Lines of communication and appropriate responsibilities should be clearly understood by all people affected by the arrangement. If possible, these should be written down and circulated.

- Payment for homeworking may be based on output (work completed) rather than input (hours worked) and, if so, this should be clearly established at the outset.

- The employer remains responsible for the employee's health and safety while working at home.

- The employer remains responsible for the protection of any data used and processed by the employee.

- The employer must inspect the employee's place and working arrangements to ensure that the employer's equipment and data are properly safeguarded and that appropriate separation has been established between work and domestic arrangements.

- There should be an inventory of items belonging to the employer that are kept at the employee's home.

- Workload and performance standards should be equivalent to those of comparable workers at the employer's place of business.

- Homeworkers should be provided with an appropriate payslip, just like other workers.

It may suit both parties for the employee to become self-employed. If this is the case, then a contract for service, as opposed to an employment contract of service, should be prepared allowing both parties to be fully aware of, and in agreement with, the working arrangements. Having said this, it is essential for the self-employment to be genuine or else the Inland Revenue will come down like a ton of bricks on the employer.

Tax

There won't be many alterations to your tax position if you work from home. However, it would not go amiss for me to include the sort of things an employee can claim against tax. It is not a very long list, but your changed circumstances may have created some expenses that you may be able to claim.

Business expenses

If you are an employee, which business expenses are deductible for tax purposes and which are not?

Clothes

Normally allowed: The cost of replacing, cleaning and repairing protective clothing (e.g. overalls, boots) and functional clothing (e.g. uniforms) necessary for your job and which you are required to provide. The cost of cleaning protective clothing or functional clothing provided by your employer, if cleaning facilities are not provided.

Not allowed: Ordinary clothes you wear for work (e.g. pinstripe suit) which you could wear outside work – even if you never choose to.

Tools, etc.

Normally allowed: The cost of maintaining and repairing tools and instruments which you are required to provide. The cost of replacing tools and instruments.

Not allowed: The initial cost of tools and instruments, but you may be able to claim capital allowances (see page 35 for more information).

Cost of working at home

Normally allowed: A proportion of lighting, heating, telephone, cleaning, insurance, rent, Council Tax and water rates if part of the home is used exclusively for business. However, these expenses are only allowed if it is necessary that you carry out your duties at or from home (i.e. if it is an express or implied condition of your employment). Claiming Council Tax, water rates or ground rent may mean some Capital Gains Tax to pay if you sell your home, but this is unlikely.

Working from Home

Stationery, etc.

Normally allowed: The cost of reference books which are necessary for your job and which you are required to provide. The cost of stationery used strictly for your job.

Not allowed: The cost of books you feel you need to do your job properly but which are, in fact, unnecessary, as well as subscriptions to journals to keep up with general news.

Interest

Normally allowed: The interest on loans to buy equipment (e.g. a personal computer) necessary for the job.

Not allowed: The interest on an overdraft or credit card.

Travelling

Normally allowed: Expenses incurred strictly in the course of carrying out the job. A company car, if you pay for running costs (e.g. petrol, repairs, maintenance), and you can claim a proportion of the cost for business mileage.

Not allowed: Travel to and from work. The cost of buying a car.

Accompanying spouses

Normally allowed: The cost of your spouse travelling with you if he or she has, and uses, a practical qualification directly associated with the trip. Often only a proportion of the cost is allowed.

Hotels and meals

Normally allowed: If you keep up a permanent home, reasonable hotel and meal expenses when travelling in the course of your job.

Others

Normally allowed: Pension scheme contributions.

Insurance

It is important to check with your insurance company to make sure that what you are now going to be doing at home does not adversely affect your insurance cover, whether for the house, the car, the contents, public liability, etc.

Health and safety

It is the employer's duty to ensure that you are covered in your home for health and safety issues to the same extent as workers in the normal place of business. An employer must undertake a risk assessment of your work activities at home, as well as make sure that the premises is safe for any visitors. Under the Health and Safety (First Aid) Regulations 1981, he must also provide you with adequate first aid supplies in case of an accident.

In return, you will need to play your part by co-operating with your employer. It is your duty to report any faults which may be a danger to you or your visitors' safety. You may, under the Trade Union Reform and Employment Rights Act 1993, stop working if you feel that you are in serious or imminent danger and this will not affect your employment rights.

Health and Safety Executive inspectors are allowed to visit you at home and can investigate and settle complaints regarding adverse working conditions at home.

An outline of the steps your employer must take to protect you when you work at home are listed in Appendix 9 and health and safety issues are also covered on page 45.

Appendices

Appendix 1

Tax rates and allowances for 2005/06

Income Tax		Taxable Income		
	Band	From	to	Rate
	2,020	0	2,090	10%
	30,310	2,091	32,400	22%
	over	32,400		40%

Capital Gains Tax (for individuals)		First	8,500	Exempt
		Balance taxed at 20% and/or 40%		
	Taper relief for long-term gains. This is now complicated – consult an accountant for details.			

Corporation Tax	Band	From	to	Rate
	10,000	0	10,000	0%
	40,000	10,001	50,000	23.75%
	250,000	50,001	300,000	19%
	1,200,000	300,001	1,500,000	32.75%
	over	1,500,001		30%

Inheritance Tax (on death)	Band	From	to	Rate
	275,000	0	275,000	0%
	over	275,000		40%

Personal Allowances		
	Personal	4,895
	Personal (aged 65 to 74)	7,090
	Married Couples (65 to 74)*#	5,905
	Personal over 75	7,220
	Married Couples over 75*#	5,975

All 4 higher age allowances are only available for incomes up to £19,500 in 2005/06
* = relief restricted to 10%   # = husband or wife must be born before 6 April 1937

National Insurance Class 1 (Employment)		
	Employee (not contracted out)	
	Earnings per week	
	Up to £94	Nil
	£94 to £630	11%
	Over £630	1%
	Employer (not contracted out)	
	Up to £94	Nil
	Over £94	12.8%

Class 2 (Self-Employment)	(The old weekly stamp)	£2.10
	No contributions due if profits below £4,345	

Class 4 (Self-Employment)	8% on profits between	£4,895	and	£32,760
	1% on profits over £32,760			

State Pension		Week	Year
	Single	82.05	£4,266.60
	Married	131.20	£6,822.40
	Over 80	0.25	£13.00

VAT	Threshold with effect from 1 April 2005	£60,000
	Rate	17.5%

Quarterly Scale Charge for Motoring			Engine Size	
		to 1400cc	1401–2000	over 2000
	Fuel Petrol	36.64	46.32	68.08
	Diesel	35.15	35.15	44.68

Taxable Car Benefits	The taxable Fuel Benefit is the same percentage as the Car Benefit, and applied to £14,400.
	Car Benefit is now based on CO_2 emissions.
	Visit www.inlandrevenue.gov.uk to find out how to calculate Car and Fuel Benefits.

		Age at End of Tax Year	
		Less than 4 years old	Over 4 years old
	Vans	£500	£350

Car Mileage Allowance	All Engine Sizes
Up to 10,000 miles pa	40p
Over 10,000 miles pa	25p

Working from Home

Appendix 1 (continued)

Tax rates and allowances for 2004/05

<table>
<tr><td>Income Tax</td><td></td><td>Taxable Income
From</td><td>to</td><td>Rate</td></tr>
<tr><td></td><td>2,020</td><td>0</td><td>2,020</td><td>10%</td></tr>
<tr><td></td><td>29,380</td><td>2,021</td><td>31,400</td><td>22%</td></tr>
<tr><td></td><td>over</td><td>31,400</td><td></td><td>40%</td></tr>
</table>

<table>
<tr><td>Capital Gains Tax
(for individuals)</td><td>First</td><td>8,200</td><td>Exempt</td></tr>
<tr><td></td><td colspan="3">Balance taxed at 20% and/or 40%</td></tr>
<tr><td></td><td colspan="3">Taper relief for long-term gains. This is now complicated – consult an accountant for details.</td></tr>
</table>

<table>
<tr><td>Corporation Tax</td><td>Band</td><td>From</td><td>to</td><td>Rate</td></tr>
<tr><td></td><td>10,000</td><td>0</td><td>10,000</td><td>0%</td></tr>
<tr><td></td><td>40,000</td><td>10,001</td><td>50,000</td><td>23.75%</td></tr>
<tr><td></td><td>250,000</td><td>50,001</td><td>300,000</td><td>19%</td></tr>
<tr><td></td><td>1,200,000</td><td>300,001</td><td>1,500,000</td><td>32.75%</td></tr>
<tr><td></td><td>over</td><td>1,500,001</td><td></td><td>30%</td></tr>
</table>

<table>
<tr><td>Inheritance Tax
(on death)</td><td>Band</td><td>From</td><td>to</td><td>Rate</td></tr>
<tr><td></td><td>263,000</td><td>0</td><td>263,000</td><td>0%</td></tr>
<tr><td></td><td>over</td><td>263,000</td><td></td><td>40%</td></tr>
</table>

<table>
<tr><td>Personal Allowances</td><td>Personal</td><td>4,745</td></tr>
<tr><td></td><td>Personal (aged 65 to 74)</td><td>6,830</td></tr>
<tr><td></td><td>Married Couples (66 to 74)*#</td><td>5,725</td></tr>
<tr><td></td><td>Personal over 75</td><td>6,950</td></tr>
<tr><td></td><td>Married Couples over 75*#</td><td>5,795</td></tr>
<tr><td></td><td colspan="2">All 4 higher age allowances are only available for incomes up to £18,900 in 2004/05
* = relief restricted to 10%   # = husband or wife must be born before 6 April 1937</td></tr>
</table>

<table>
<tr><td>National Insurance
Class 1 (Employment)</td><td>Employee (not contracted out)
Earnings per week</td><td></td></tr>
<tr><td></td><td>Up to £91</td><td>Nil</td></tr>
<tr><td></td><td>£91 to £610</td><td>11%</td></tr>
<tr><td></td><td>Over £610</td><td>1%</td></tr>
<tr><td></td><td>Employer (not contracted out)</td><td></td></tr>
<tr><td></td><td>Up to £91</td><td>Nil</td></tr>
<tr><td></td><td>Over £91</td><td>12.8%</td></tr>
</table>

<table>
<tr><td>Class 2 (Self-Employment)</td><td>(The old weekly stamp)</td><td></td><td></td><td>£2.05</td></tr>
<tr><td></td><td colspan="4">No contributions due if profits below £4,215</td></tr>
</table>

<table>
<tr><td>Class 4 (Self-Employment)</td><td>8% on profits between</td><td>£4,745</td><td>and</td><td>£31,720</td></tr>
<tr><td></td><td colspan="4">1% on profits over £31,720</td></tr>
</table>

<table>
<tr><td>State Pension</td><td></td><td>Week</td><td>Year</td></tr>
<tr><td></td><td>Single</td><td>79.60</td><td>£4,139.20</td></tr>
<tr><td></td><td>Married</td><td>127.25</td><td>£6,617.00</td></tr>
<tr><td></td><td>Over 80</td><td>0.25</td><td>£13.00</td></tr>
</table>

<table>
<tr><td>VAT</td><td>Threshold</td><td>£58,000</td></tr>
<tr><td></td><td>Rate</td><td>17.5%</td></tr>
</table>

<table>
<tr><td>Quarterly Scale
Charge for Motoring</td><td></td><td>to 1400cc</td><td>Engine Size
1401–2000</td><td>over 2000</td></tr>
<tr><td></td><td>Fuel</td><td></td><td></td><td></td></tr>
<tr><td></td><td>Petrol</td><td>34.55</td><td>43.63</td><td>64.34</td></tr>
<tr><td></td><td>Diesel</td><td>32.17</td><td>32.17</td><td>40.65</td></tr>
</table>

<table>
<tr><td>Taxable Car Benefits</td><td>The Fuel Benefit is now based on CO_2 emissions.</td></tr>
<tr><td></td><td>The Car Benefit is now based on CO_2 emissions.
Visit www.inlandrevenue.gov.uk to find out how to calculate Car
and Fuel Benefits.</td></tr>
</table>

<table>
<tr><td></td><td colspan="2">Age at End of Tax Year</td></tr>
<tr><td></td><td>Less than 4 years old</td><td>over 4 years old</td></tr>
<tr><td></td><td>Vans</td><td>£500</td><td>£350</td></tr>
<tr><td>Car Mileage Allowance</td><td>All Engine Sizes</td><td></td></tr>
<tr><td>Up to 10,000 miles pa</td><td>40p</td><td></td></tr>
<tr><td>Over 10,000 miles pa</td><td>25p</td><td></td></tr>
</table>

Appendix 2

Some popular ways of earning money from home

- Run a business from home
- Work at home for an employer some distance away
- Bed-and-breakfast
- Lodgers
- Rent part of the house to someone else
- Let out or use your land for
  - horse shows
  - car parking
  - garden fêtes
  - flower shows
  - children's sports
  - marriage premises
  - forestry
  - wind farming
  - caravans
  - TV/film location
- Rent out an outbuilding
- Dog walking
- Child-minding
- Provide storage facilities
- Look after neighbours' houses, gardens, pets while they are away
- Provide a personalised telephone answering service for small local businesses while they are out or on holiday
- Look after someone else's elderly relative if he is left at home alone all day

Appendix 3

Minimum wage rates

You must pay workers aged 22 and over at least £4.85 per hour (increasing to £5.05 on 1 October 2005, and to £5.35 on 1 October 2006). However, there are other rates you should know, as shown on the following table.

16–17 year olds	£3.00
18–21 year olds	£4.10 (increasing to £4.25 on 1 October 2005, and to £4.45 on 1 October 2006)

The Inland Revenue is likely to ask you to prove that you are paying at least these rates, so you must keep records. Failure may result in fines of up to £5,000 for each offence.

For more information, call the Department of Trade and Industry on 0845 845 0360 or you can check the latest rates at www.dti.gov.uk/er/nmw.

Appendix 4

Sample full business plan

The following is a suggested layout of an elementary business plan:

1. *Amount of money required and how it will be used*
   Give very brief details of purpose, to introduce the reader to your needs. Also mention here the security you have available.

2. *Products or services*
   (a) Existing (if any).
       Say when the business was established.
       Give description (including standard publicity and handouts).

   (b) Proposed.
       Give here the full details of what you are proposing to do.

3. *Names of professional advisers*
   Mention accountants/auditors, solicitors, bankers, stockbrokers, design and marketing consultants. Give their contact details as an attachment to the report and state which of them have been consulted in preparing the report.

4. *Audited accounts (if relevant)*
   Attach accounts for at least the previous two years or a shorter period if the business is younger. If the latest accounts are not finalised, include figures subject to audit.

5. *Information on current trading position (if relevant)*
   Attach:
   (a) Management accounts comparing actual and budget for both revenue and capital.
   (b) Cashflow compared to budget.
   (c) Comments on variation.

6. *Forecasts*
   Show forecasts and projections for existing business for subsequent years with existing products and existing finances.

7. *Forecasts to show the impact of the new venture or business expansion*
   Demonstrate exactly when and how borrowings will be repaid.

8. *Market research*
   Mention briefly findings and conclusion of report.

9. *Competition*
   Briefly comment on competitors.

10. *Major customers*
    Identify them and indicate level of interest in project, product or expansion as the case may be.

11. *Major suppliers*
    Identify and mention reliability.

12. *Production and distribution plans*
    Refer to separate report if relevant and changes that are to be made.

13. *Contingencies*
    Build into forecasts any likely risks and how they have been allowed for (e.g. 'We hope the product will be launched in September, but we are allowing for a delay until December.').

Appendix 5

Sample agreement when one spouse agrees to work for the other

Agreement between:

_____

and

_____.

We, the undersigned, agree that my wife/husband undertakes responsibility for the following activities in my business:

- _____
- _____
- _____
- _____
- _____
- _____

It is agreed that for these services my wife/husband will receive the sum of £_____ per year to be paid monthly. This agreement is effective from _____.

Signed: _____ Proprietor

Signed: _____ Wife/husband

Dated: _____

Appendix 6

Matters that should be included in an employment contract

- Name of employer
- Name of employee
- Date of commencement
- Job description
- Hours of work
- Rates of pay
- Holiday entitlement
- Periods of notice
- Disciplinary procedures
- Grievance procedures
- Sick pay
- Jury service
- Pension scheme details
- That home working arrangements are the subject of a separate set of regulations

Appendix 7

*Specimen layout for a set of accounts and how to present
your figures to the taxman*

Your name _____ Accounting year end _____

Self-Employment and Partnerships

Sales income　　　　　　　　　　　　　　　　　　　　　　　　　　　　　　　A

　　　less　　　　**Costs of sales,** e.g. raw materials and stocks

　　　　　　　　Construction industry subcontractors' costs

　　　　　　　　Other direct costs, e.g. packing and despatch

　　　　　　　　　　　　　　　　Total cost of sales　　　　　　　　　　　B

　　　　　　　　　　　　　Gross profit or loss A – B　　　　　　　　　　C

　　　　　　　　　　　　　　　　　　Other income　　　　　　　　　　　D

Expenditure

Employee costs
Salaries, wages, bonuses, employer's NIC, pension contributions,
casual wages, canteen costs, recruitment agency fees,
subcontractors' (unless shown above) and other wages costs

Premises costs
Rent, ground rent, rates, water, refuse, light and heat, property
insurance, security and use of home

Repairs
Repair of property, replacements, renewals, maintenance

General administrative expenses
Telephone, fax, mobile telephone, stationery, photocopying, printing,
postage, courier and computer costs, subscriptions, insurance

Motoring expenses
Petrol, servicing, licence, repairs, motor insurance, hire and
leasing, car parking, RAC/AA membership

Travel and subsistence
Rail, air, bus, etc., travel, taxis, subsistence and hotel costs

Entertainment
Staff entertaining (e.g. Christmas party), customer gifts up to £50
per person advertising your business

Advertising and promotion
Advertising, promotion, mailshots, free samples, brochures,
newsletters, trade shows, etc.

Legal and professional costs
Accountancy, legal, architects, surveyors, stocktakers' fees,
indemnity insurance

Bad debts (if already included in A above)

Interest
on bank loans, overdraft and other loans

Other finance charges
Bank charges, HP interest, credit card charges, leasing not
already included

Depreciation and losses on sale (please ask for advice)

Other items – please describe

　　　　　　　　　　　　　　Grand total of expenses　　　　　　　　　E

　　　　　　　　　　　　　　Net profit (or loss)　C + D – E

Appendix 8

'Heads of agreement' for a partnership agreement between husband and wife

This is to certify that on _____ Mr and Mrs _____ agreed to enter into a _____ partnership to be based at _____.

The essential parts of their verbal agreement are:

1. Commencement date: _____.

2. Initial capital (jointly): _____.

3. There will be no entitlement of interest on capital.

4. Accounts will be drawn up to each _____.

5. The bankers shall be _____.

6. The partnership shall be dissolved on the expiry of not less than six months' notice of dissolution given in writing by one partner to the other or by any other mutually agreed procedure.

7. The partnership shall trade under the name of _____.

8. The net profits and losses shall be shared equally.

9. A partner may, from time to time, with the agreement of the other, be paid a salary prior to establishing the figure of net profit or loss for a particular year.

Signed: _____   Signed: _____

Appendix 9

Health and safety – the elementary steps that should be taken by an employer when an employee works from home

- The employee should be issued with a separate set of terms that might apply to homeworking, such as:

  - That it is voluntary.

  - That it is flexible.

  - How many days a week the employee may work from home.

  - Who is eligible to apply to work from home.

  - What equipment will be provided by the employer.

  - Any expense allowance associated with homeworking.

  - The need, if any, for the employee to clear what is proposed with his landlord, mortgage company, insurance company, etc. and that it is the employee's responsibility to ensure that the appropriate arrangements are made in this connection and to meet any costs associated with it.

  - Where business meetings, whether with fellow employees or customers, are to be held.

  - That the employee has a duty to report any work-related accidents or illnesses that occur in the home.

  - That the employee must provide a suitable work area in his home that is secure.

- While the work may be carried out in the employee's home, it is still the employer's duty to look at what might cause harm to his homeworkers, or others, as a result of the work being done in the employee's home.

- The employer should therefore visit the employee's home to carry out a risk assessment; an assessment in which the employee should help the employer identify hazards.

- The employer should consider who, apart from the employee, might be affected by the work being done at home, including children, even unborn children, as well as disabled or elderly relatives.

- The employer should provide the employee with whatever protective equipment or clothing that might be needed.

- If the employer discovers any hazards, he needs to decide what should be done about them.

- If the employer has more than five employees, he must record his findings and give a copy to the employee.

- The employer should check the risk assessment from time to time.

Some common hazards are:

- the need to handle heavy loads – employees should be told good techniques for doing this;

- repetitive work that does not allow enough rest time;

- twisting and stooping;

- insufficient training in handling work equipment in use in the home;

- lack of maintenance of the equipment;

- protective equipment and clothing not being used;

- the lack of adequate first aid provisions;

- anything that might cause risk to the employee's health.

Index

Working from Home